Women Around the World

A COLORING BOOK ADVENTURE

THE COLORING BOOK CREATED TO HELP YOU RELAX AND TAKE YOU TO SOME
SPECIAL PLACES AROUND THE WORLD.

WRITTEN AND ILLUSTRATED BY:
CHELSEA FARRELL
© COULEUR PAR BIRDIE

ISBN: 978-0-359-65503-8   (PAPERBACK)

FRONT COVER IMAGE BY CHELSEA FARRELL
BOOK DESIGN BY CHELSEA FARRELL

PRINTED BY LULU.COM, IN THE UNITED STATES OF AMERICA.

FIRST PRINTING EDITION 2019

627 DAVIS DRIVE, SUITE 300, NC 27560 MORRISVILLE, UNITED STATES

Special Note From the Author

FROM A YOUNG AGE, I WAS ALWAYS FILLED WITH CHILD-LIKE WONDERMENT. MANY ADULTS HAVE LOST THIS OVER THE YEARS.

HOWEVER, I BELIEVE THAT ADULTS CAN AND SHOULD HAVE THE SAME WONDERMENT. WHETHER OR NOT YOU CONSIDER YOURSELF AN ARTIST, THIS BOOK IS FOR YOU! THIS BOOK IS MEANT TO OUTLINE A VISION SO THAT MEANS ALL YOU NEED TO DO IS SIT BACK, GRAB A SNACK, AND COLOR THE WORLD AND ALL OF ITS BEAUTY AS YOU SEE FIT.

THIS BOOK IS MADE UP OF 25 PAGES OF COMPLETELY HAND-DRAWN ART INSPIRED BY MANY COUNTRIES AND STATES AROUND THE WORLD AND THE AMAZING WOMEN WHO INHABIT THEM.

RELAX AND ENJOY

This book belongs to:

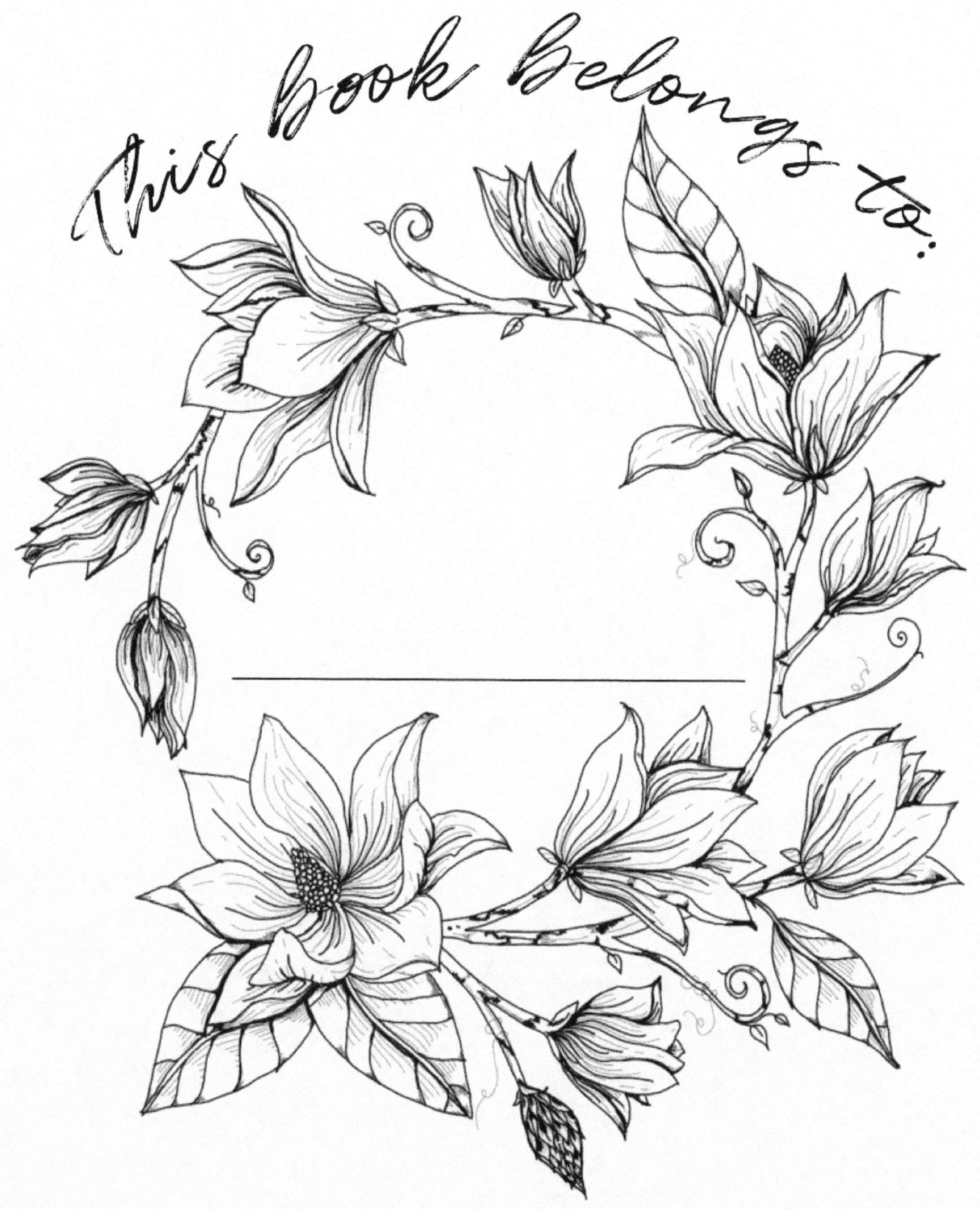

TEST COLORS HERE

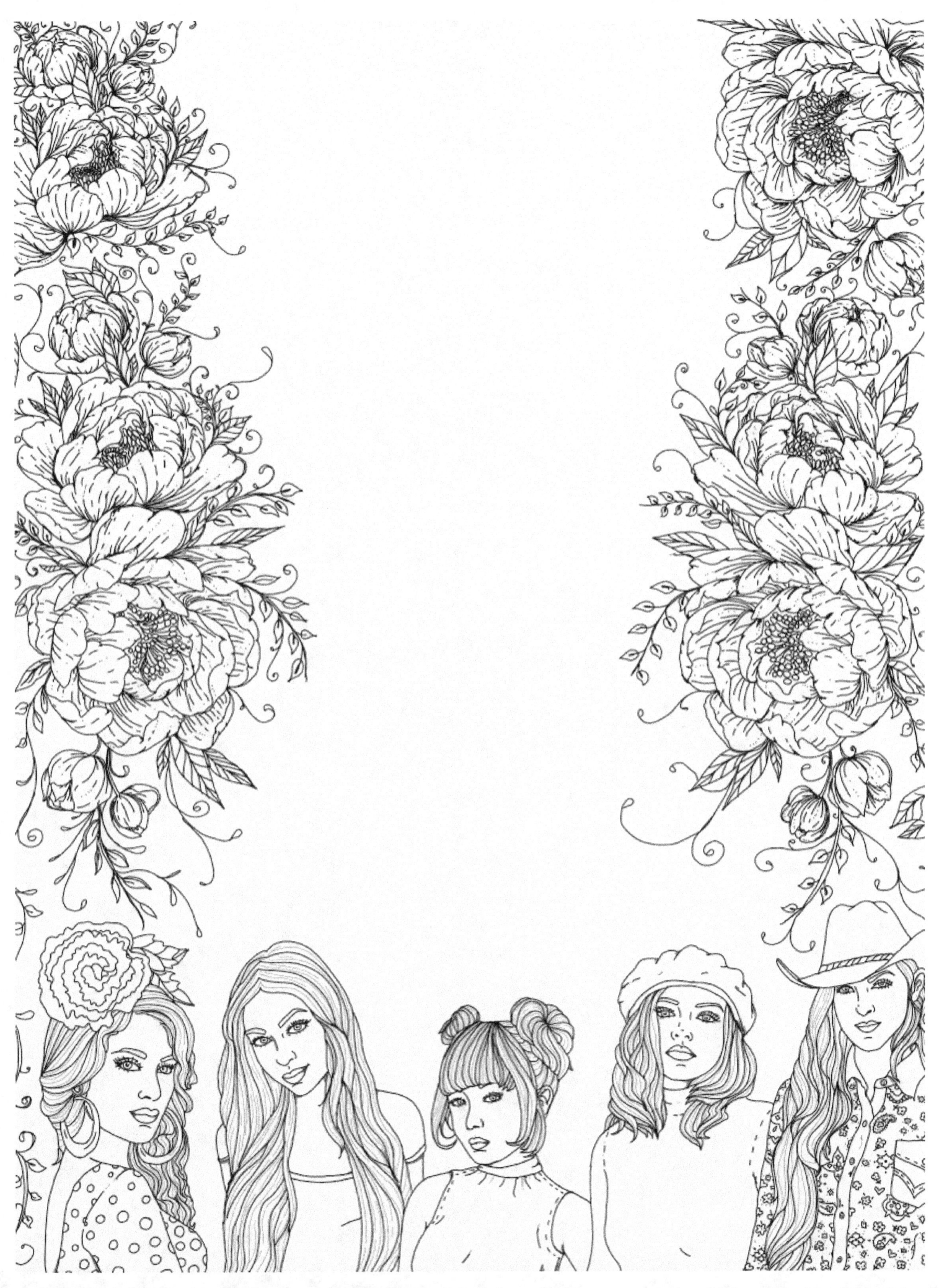

INSPIRED BY TEXAS, USA

TEST COLORS HERE

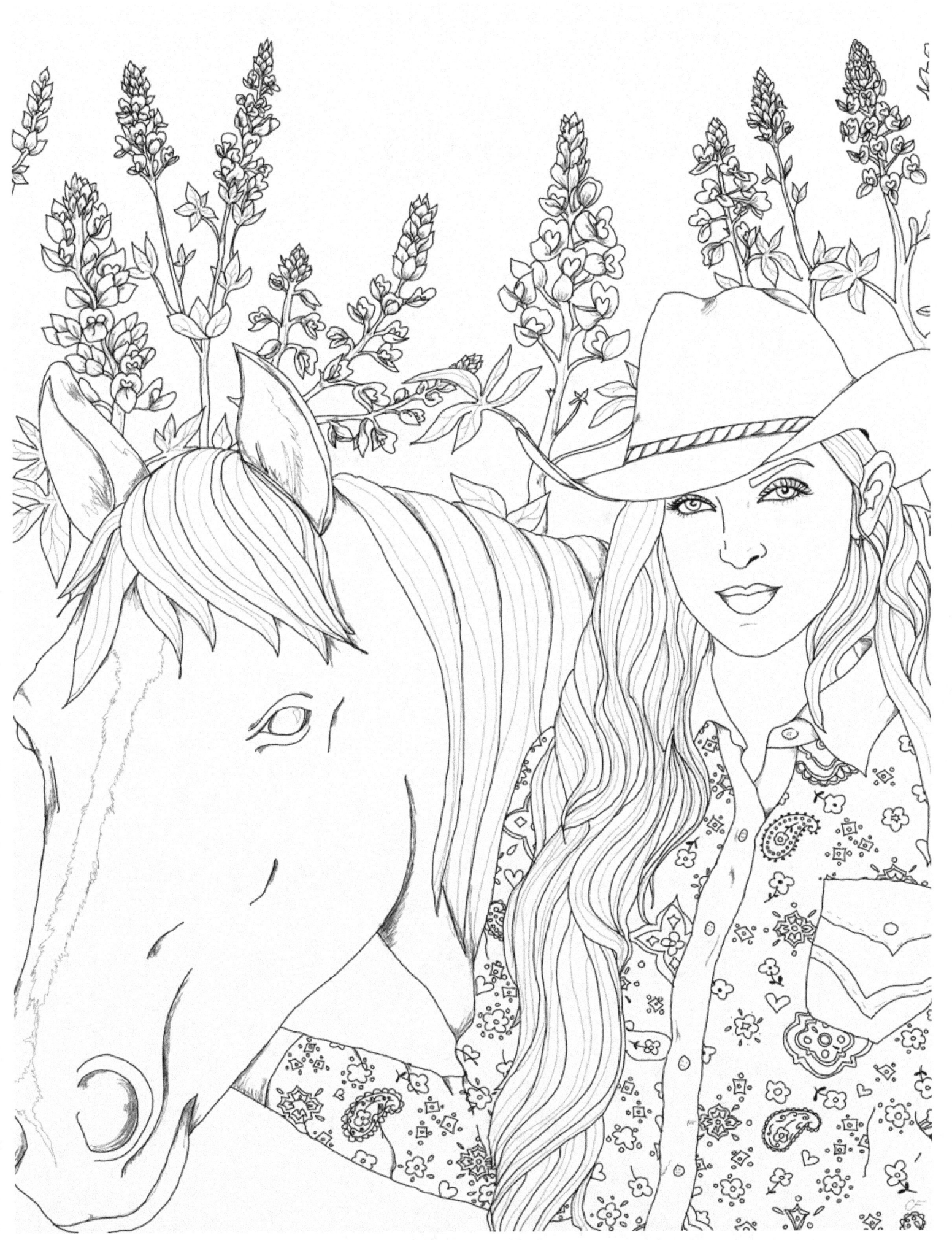

INSPIRED BY MEXICO

TEST COLORS HERE

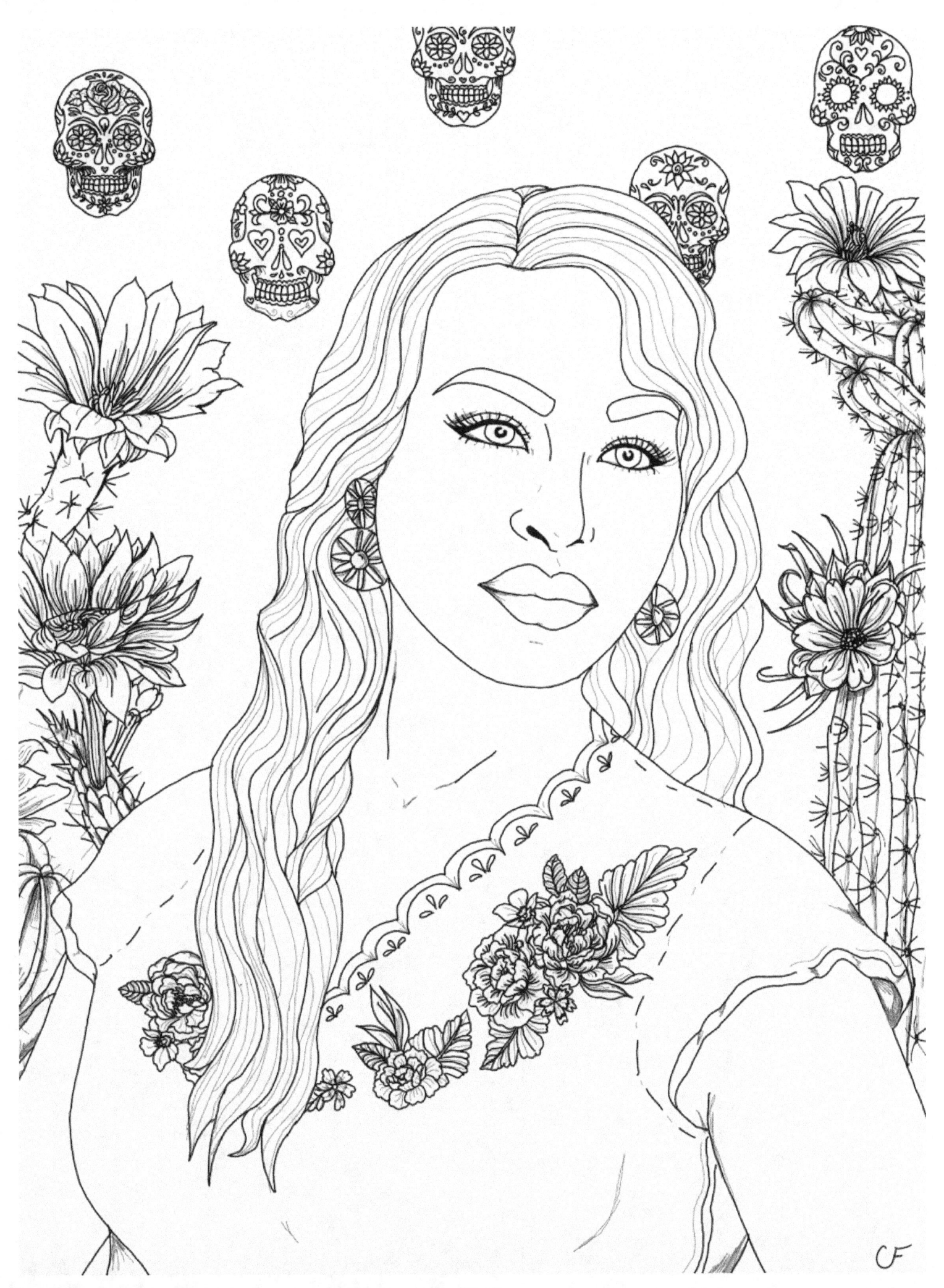

INSPIRED BY FRANCE

TEST COLORS HERE

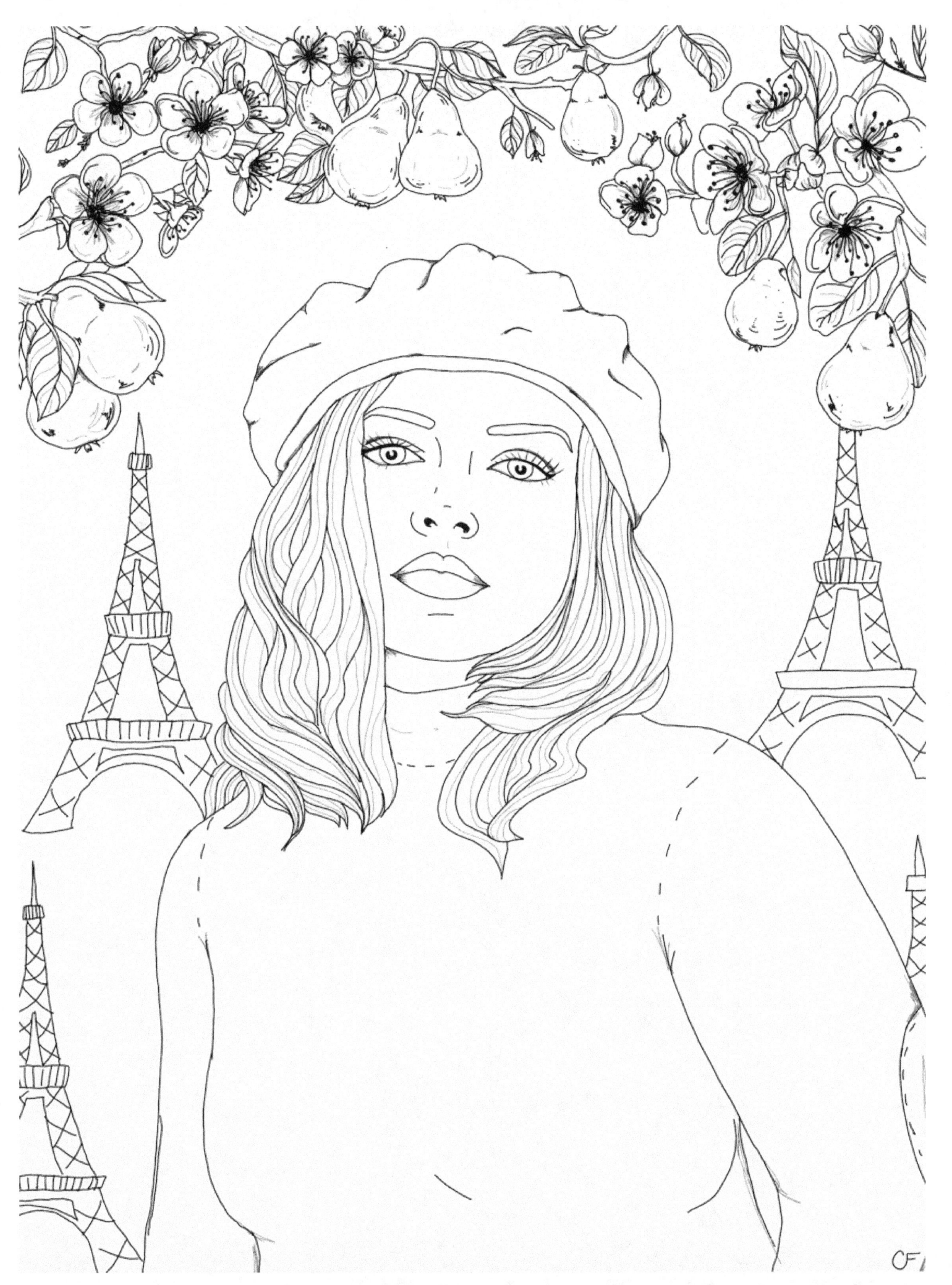

INSPIRED BY HAWAII

TEST COLORS HERE

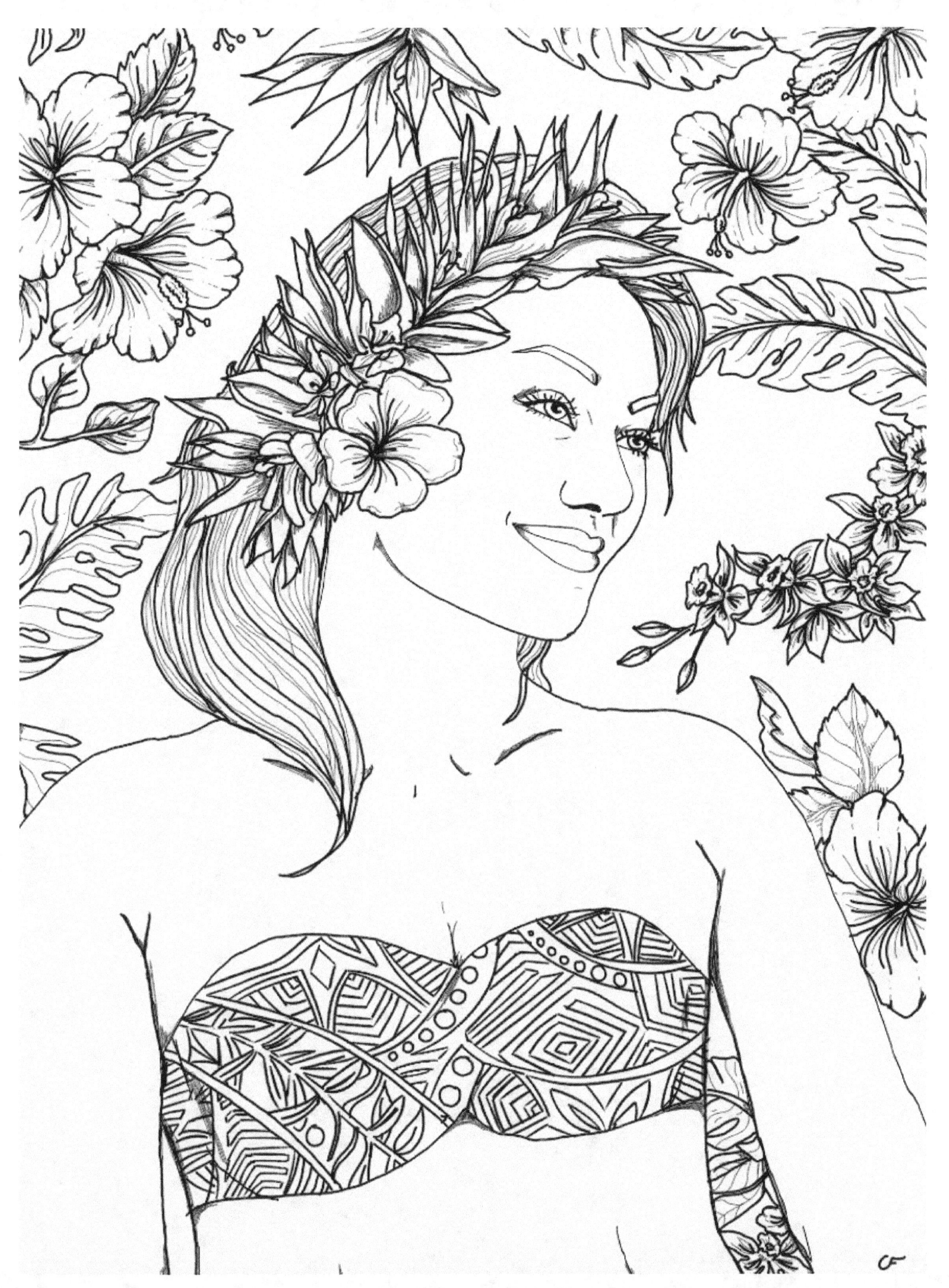

INSPIRED BY THAILAND
TEST COLORS HERE

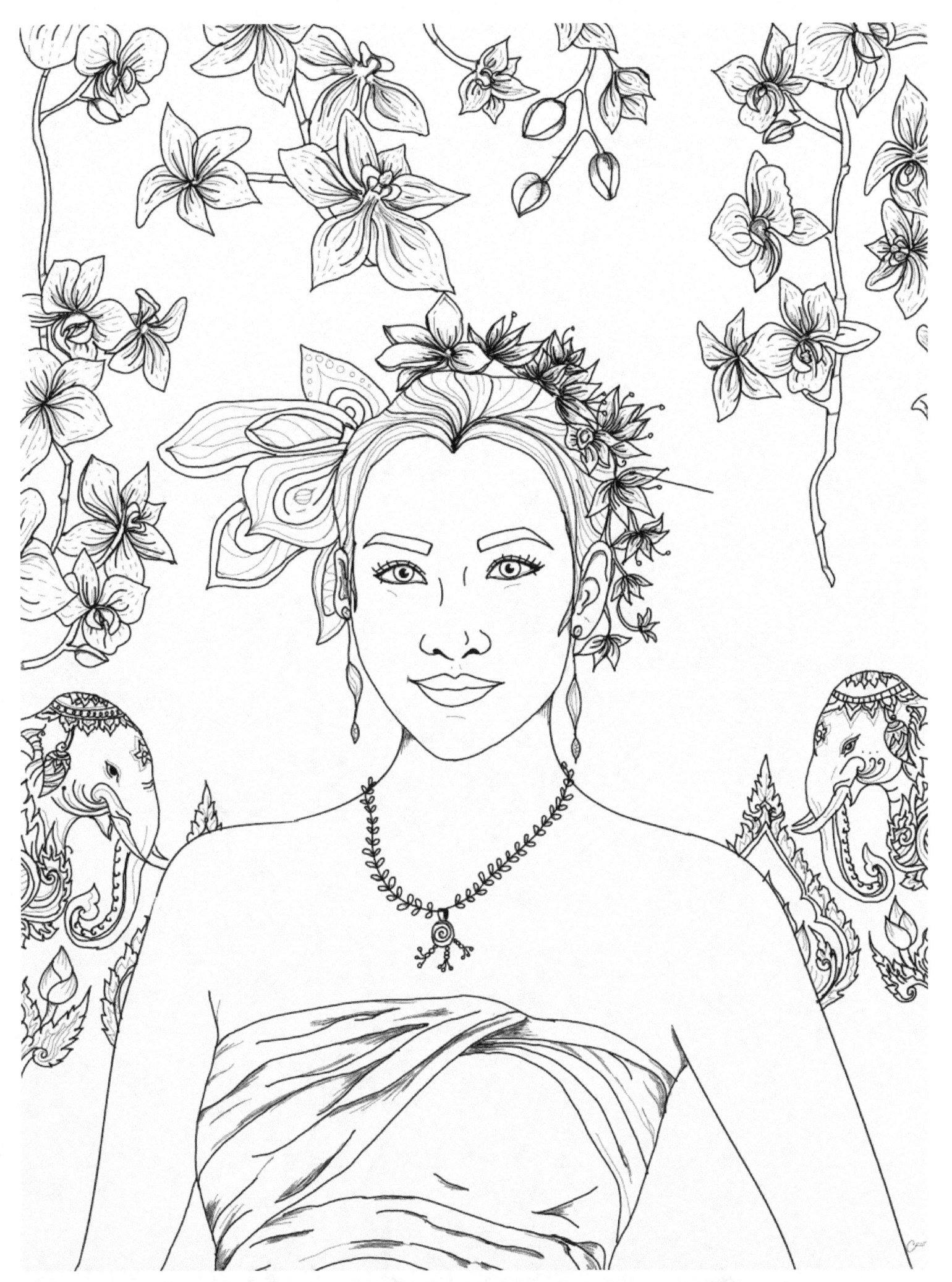

INSPIRED BY INDIA
TEST COLORS HERE

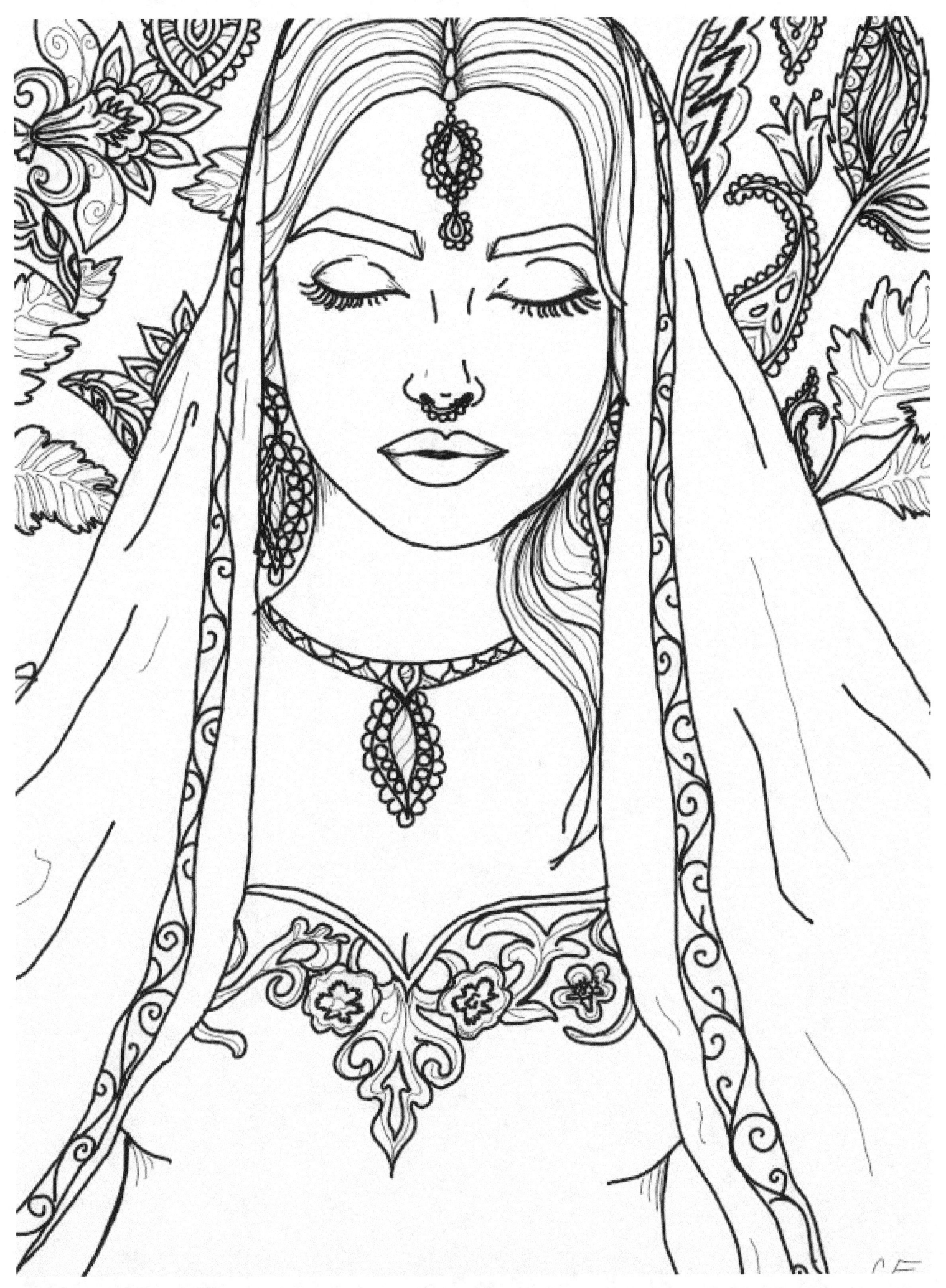

INSPIRED BY CANADA

TEST COLORS HERE

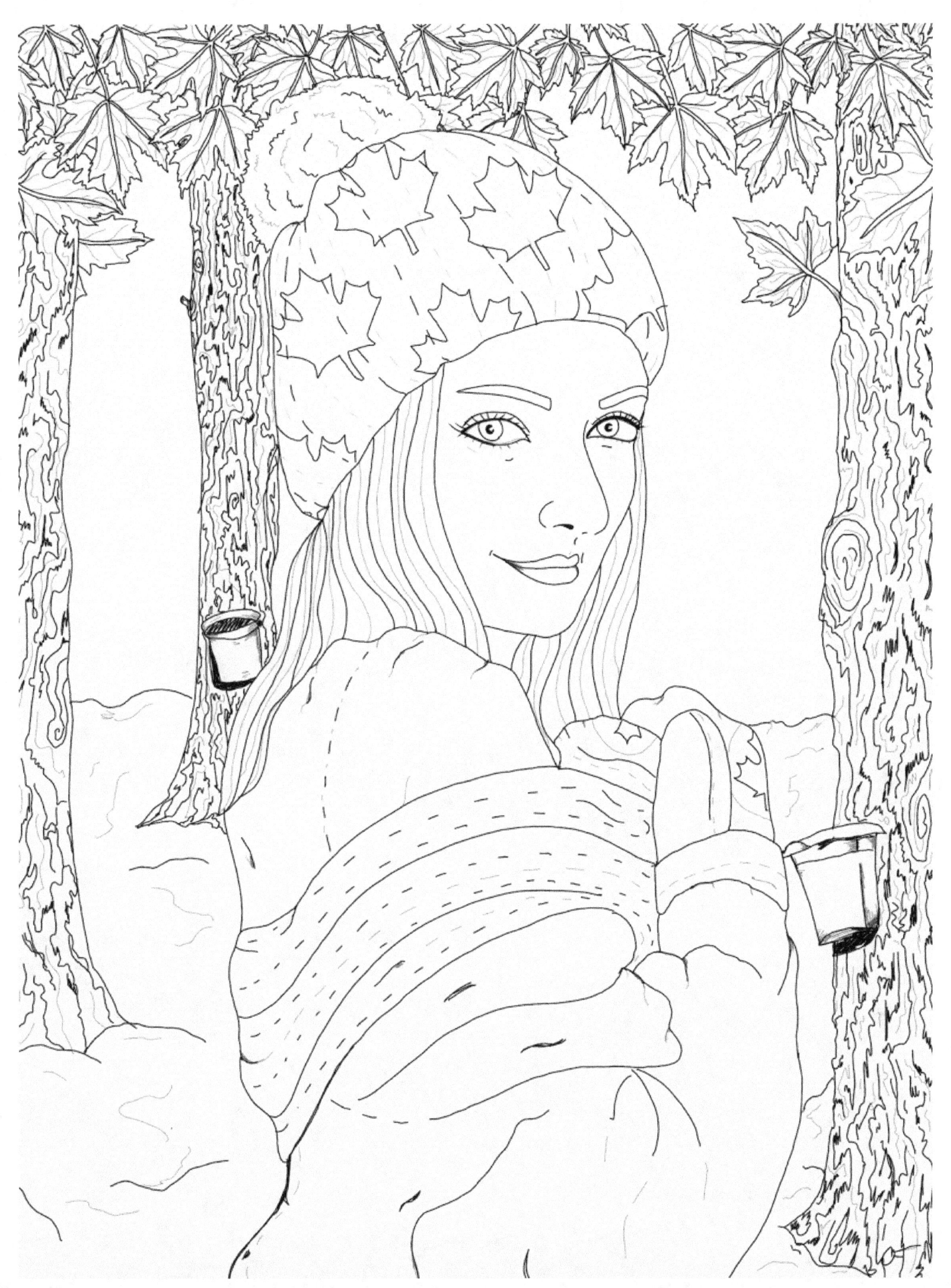

INSPIRED BY PERU

TEST COLORS HERE

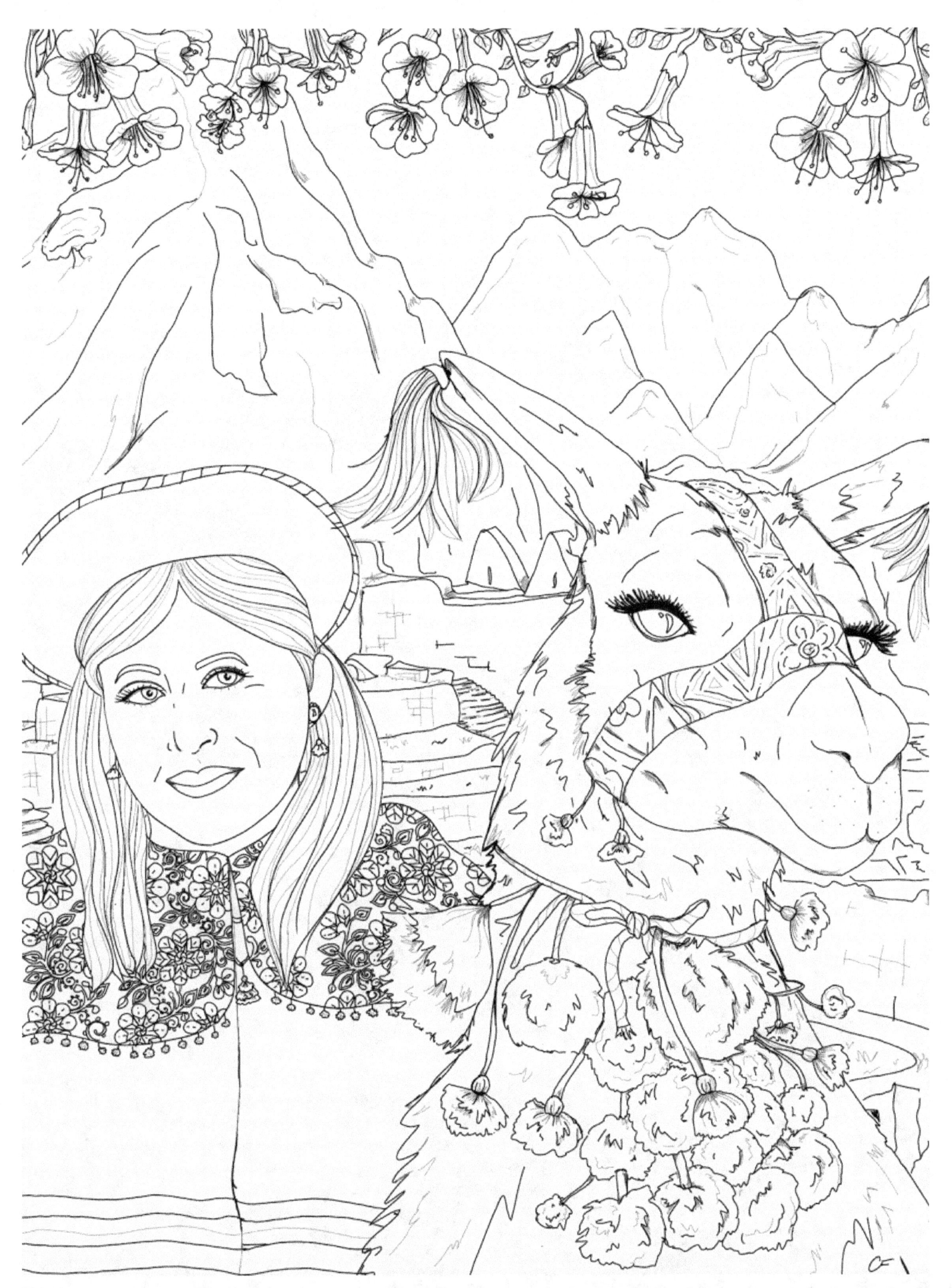

INSPIRED BY ITALY

TEST COLORS HERE

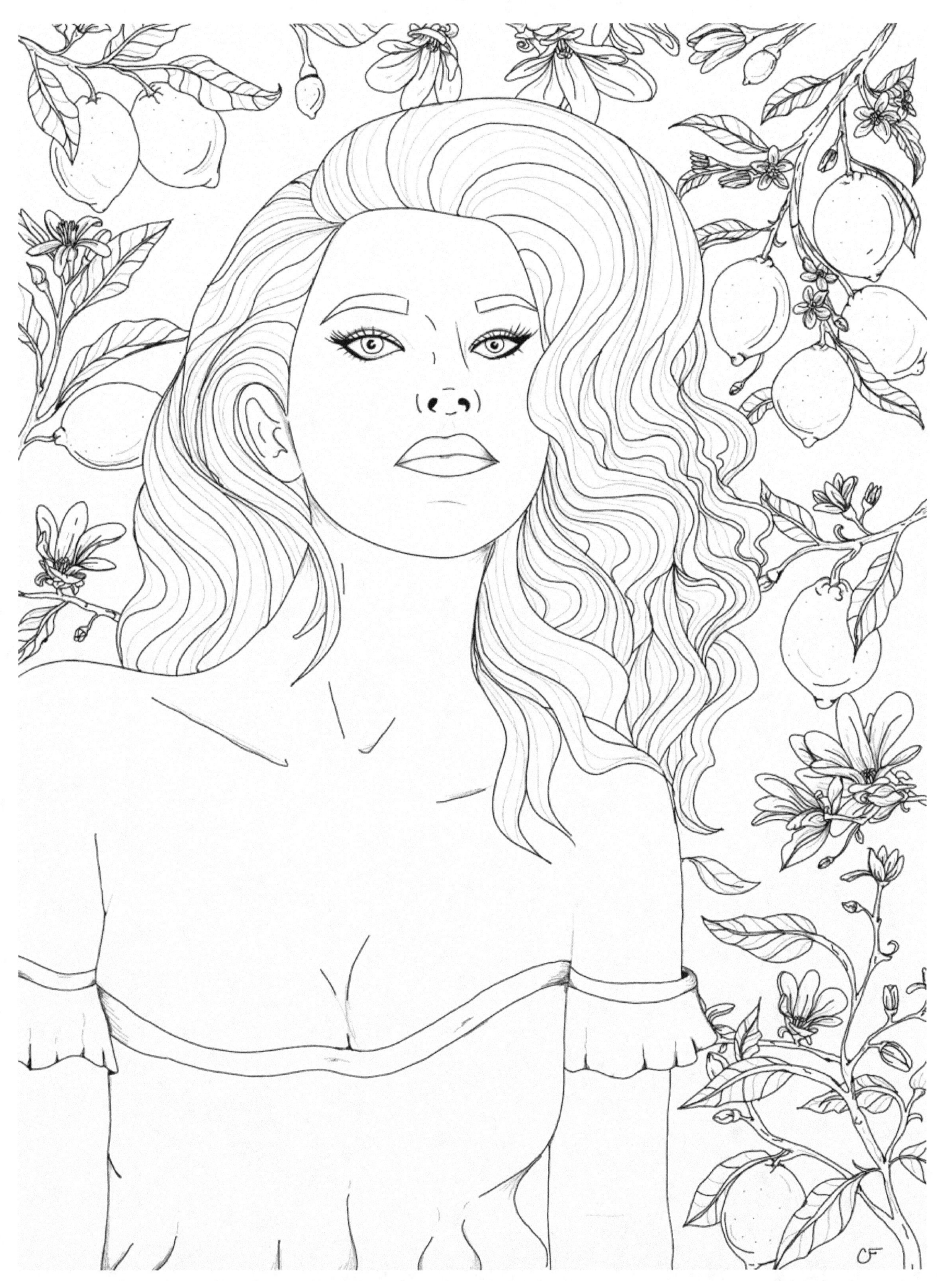

INSPIRED BY RUSSIA

TEST COLORS HERE

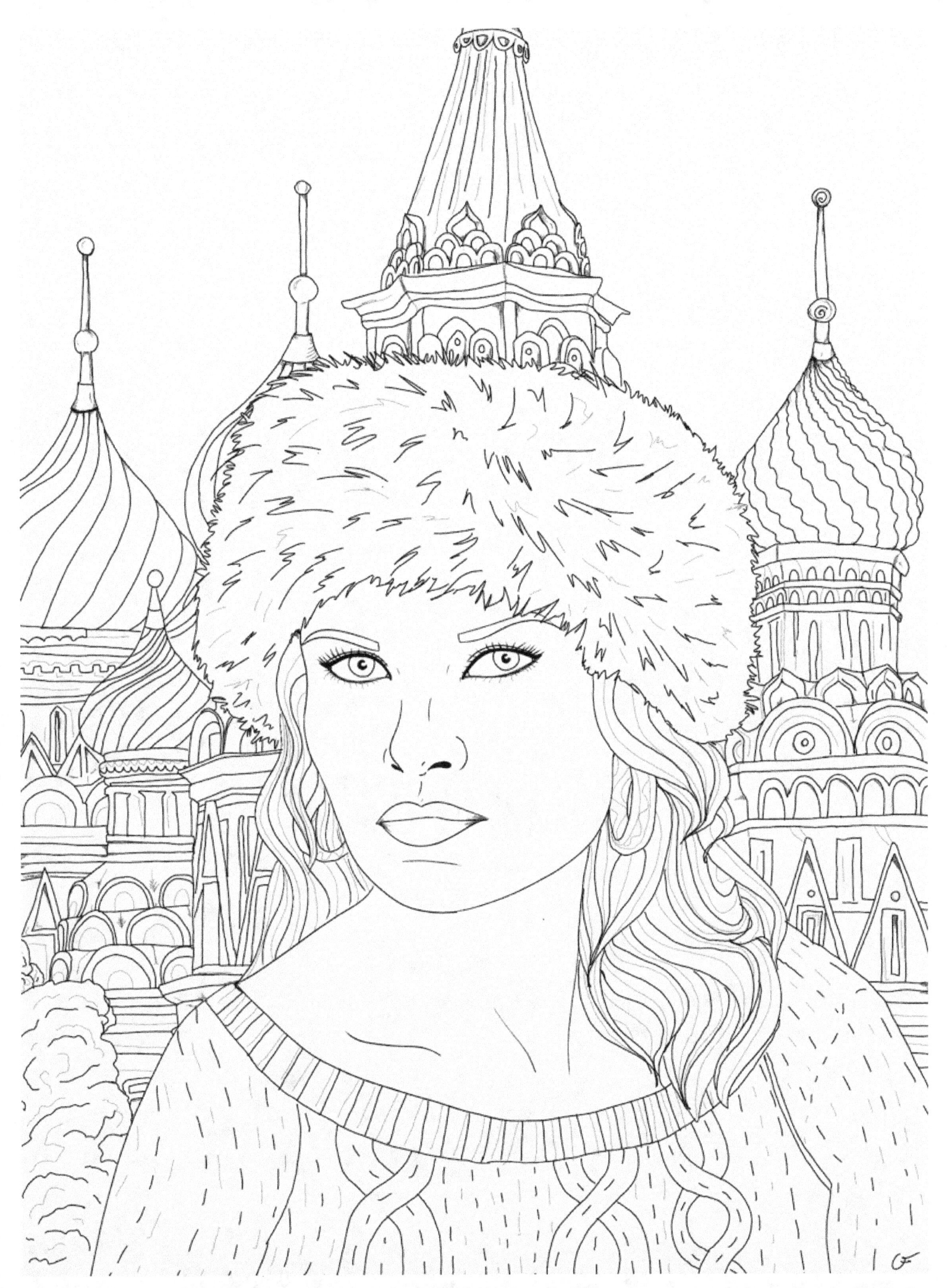

INSPIRED BY MOROCCO

TEST COLORS HERE

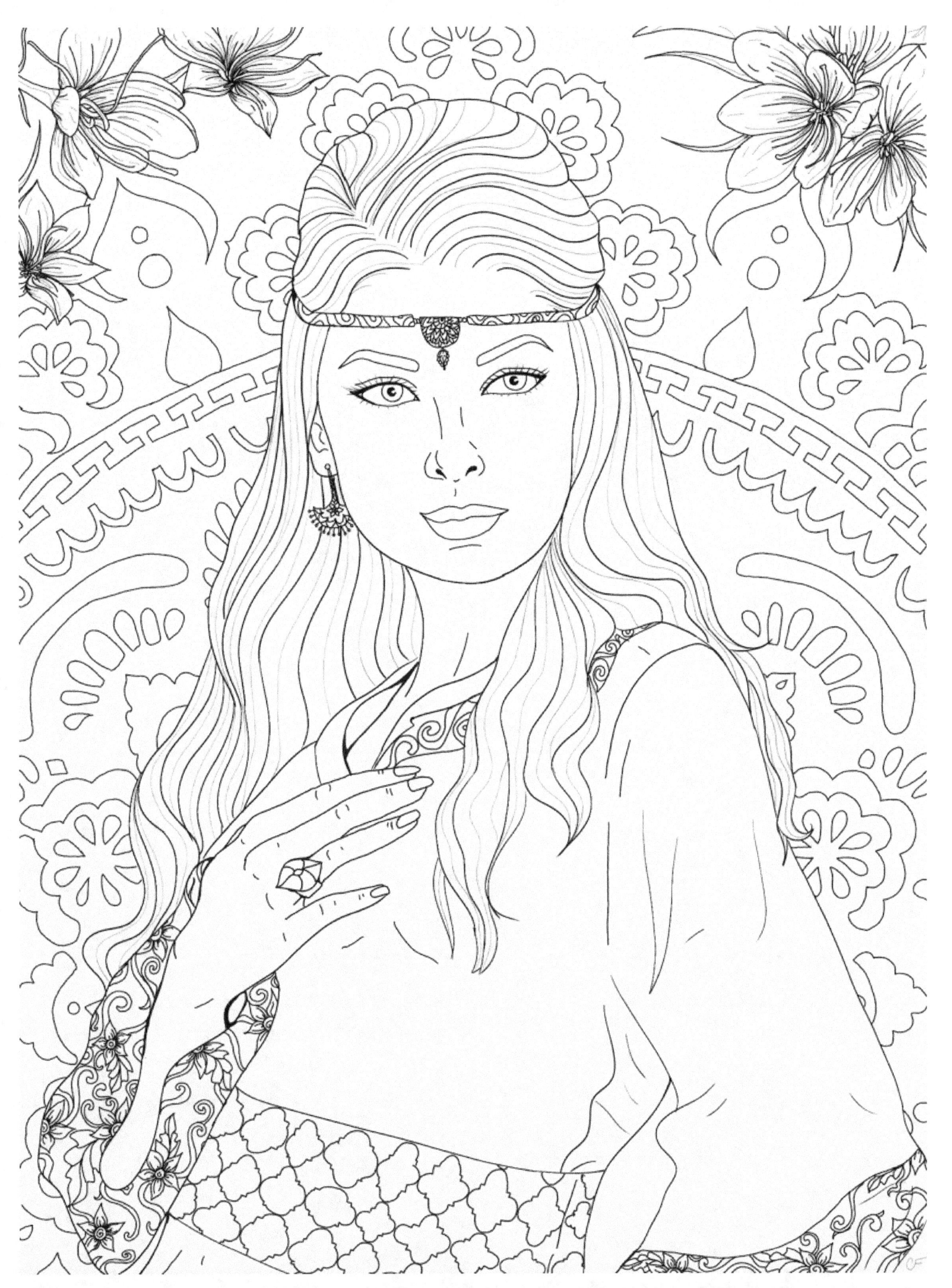

INSPIRED BY NEW YORK, USA

TEST COLORS HERE

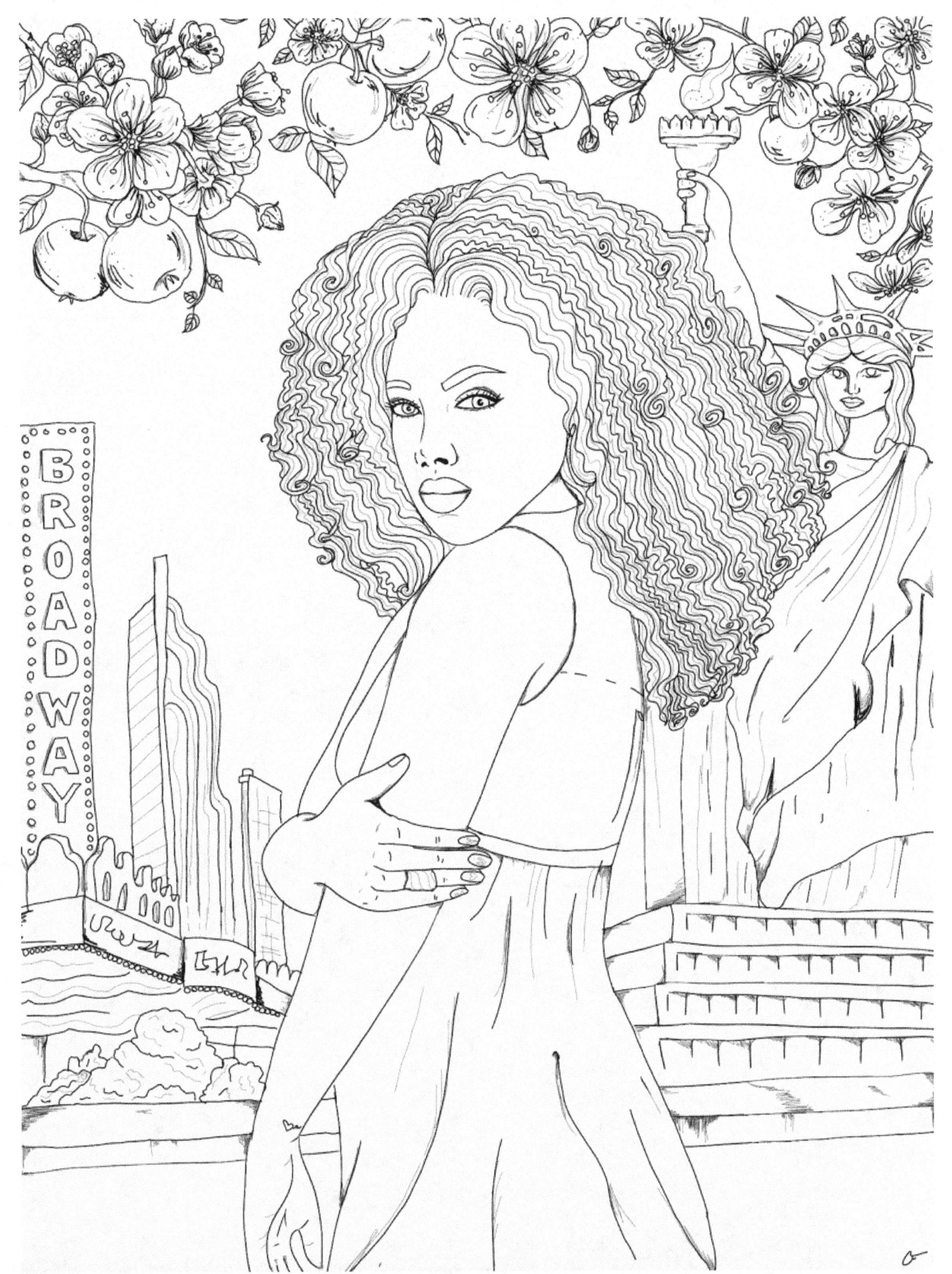

INSPIRED BY SOUTH AFRICA
TEST COLORS HERE

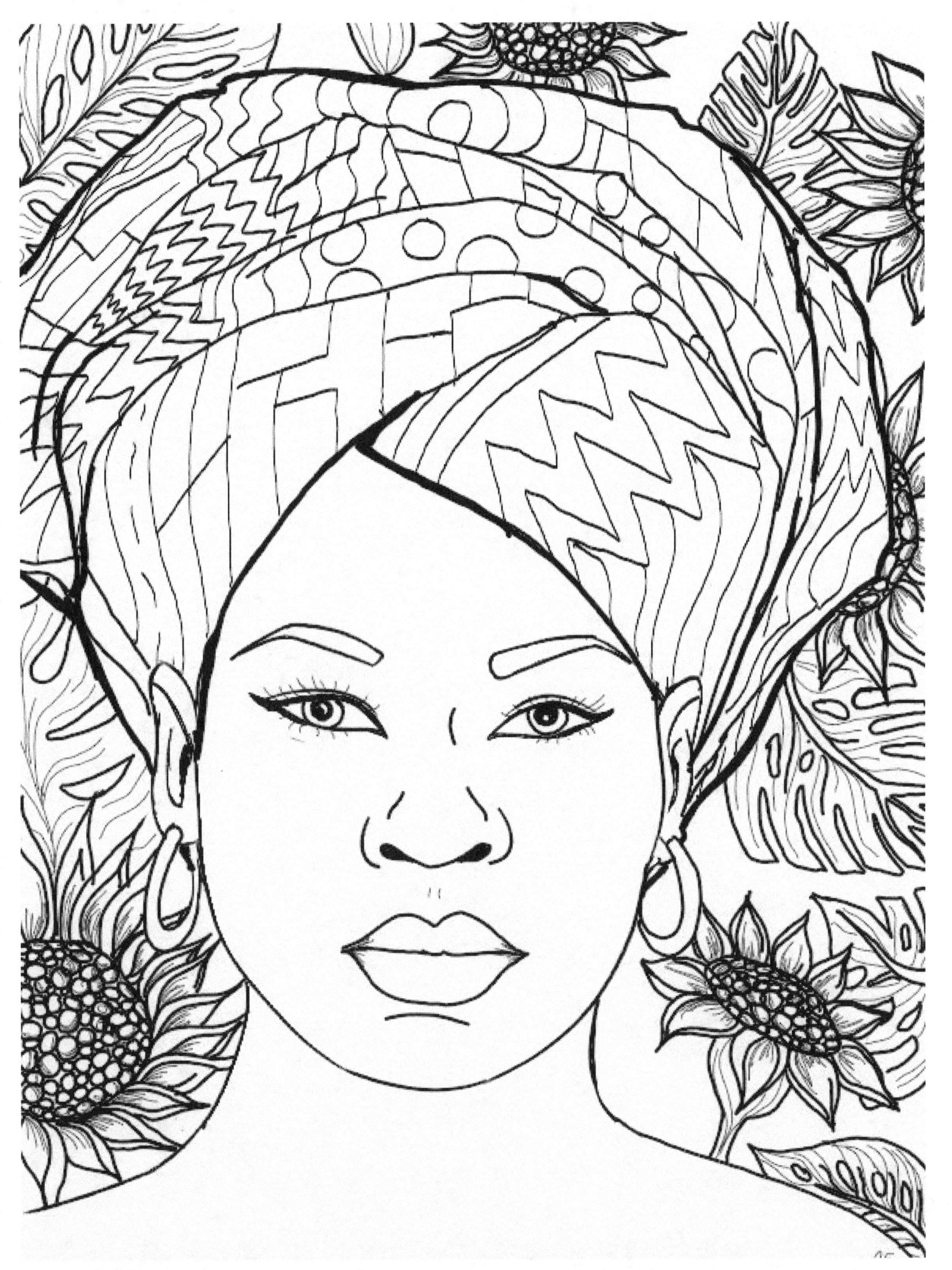

INSPIRED BY BRAZIL
TEST COLORS HERE

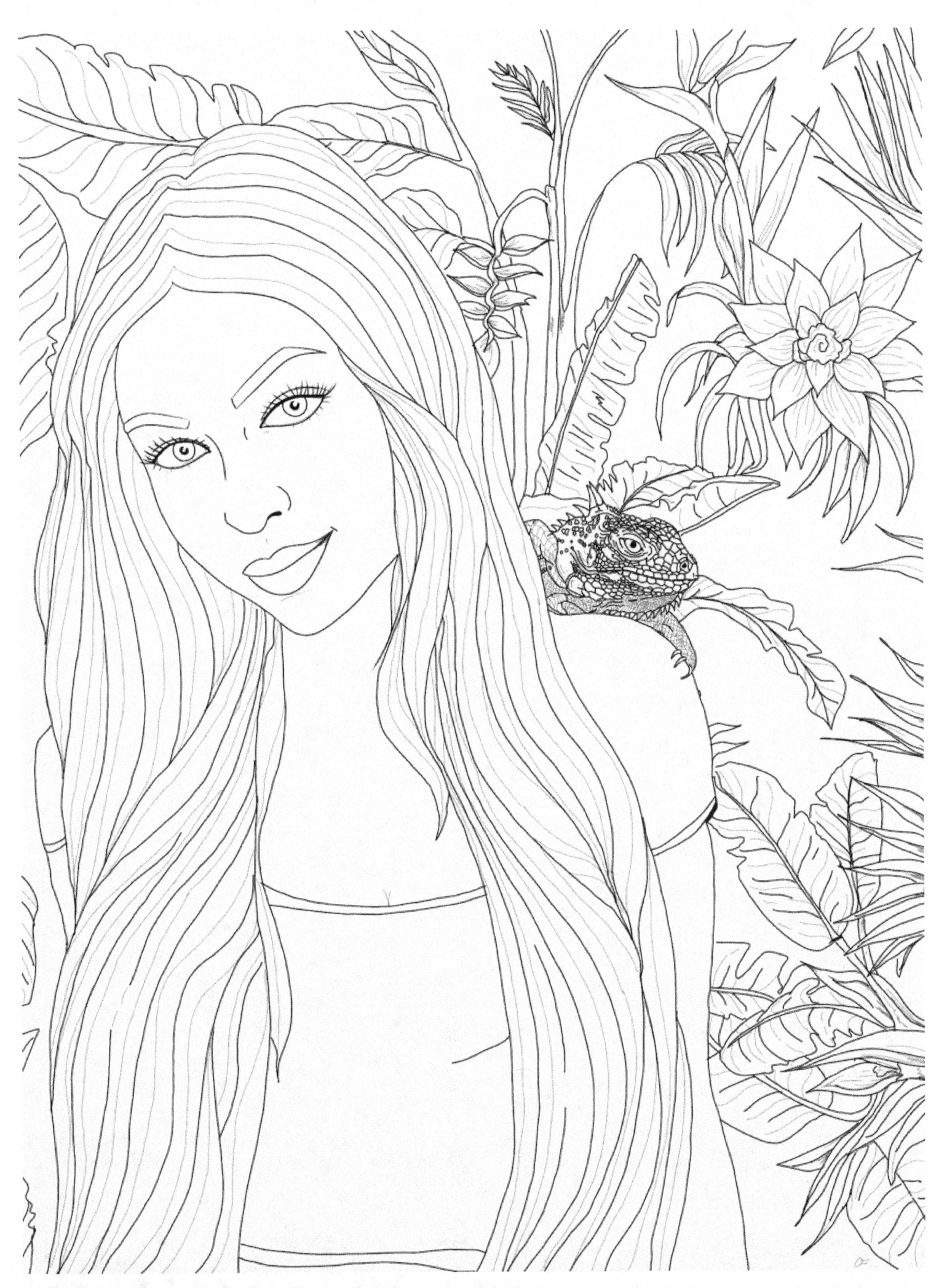

INSPIRED BY LAS VEGAS, USA

TEST COLORS HERE

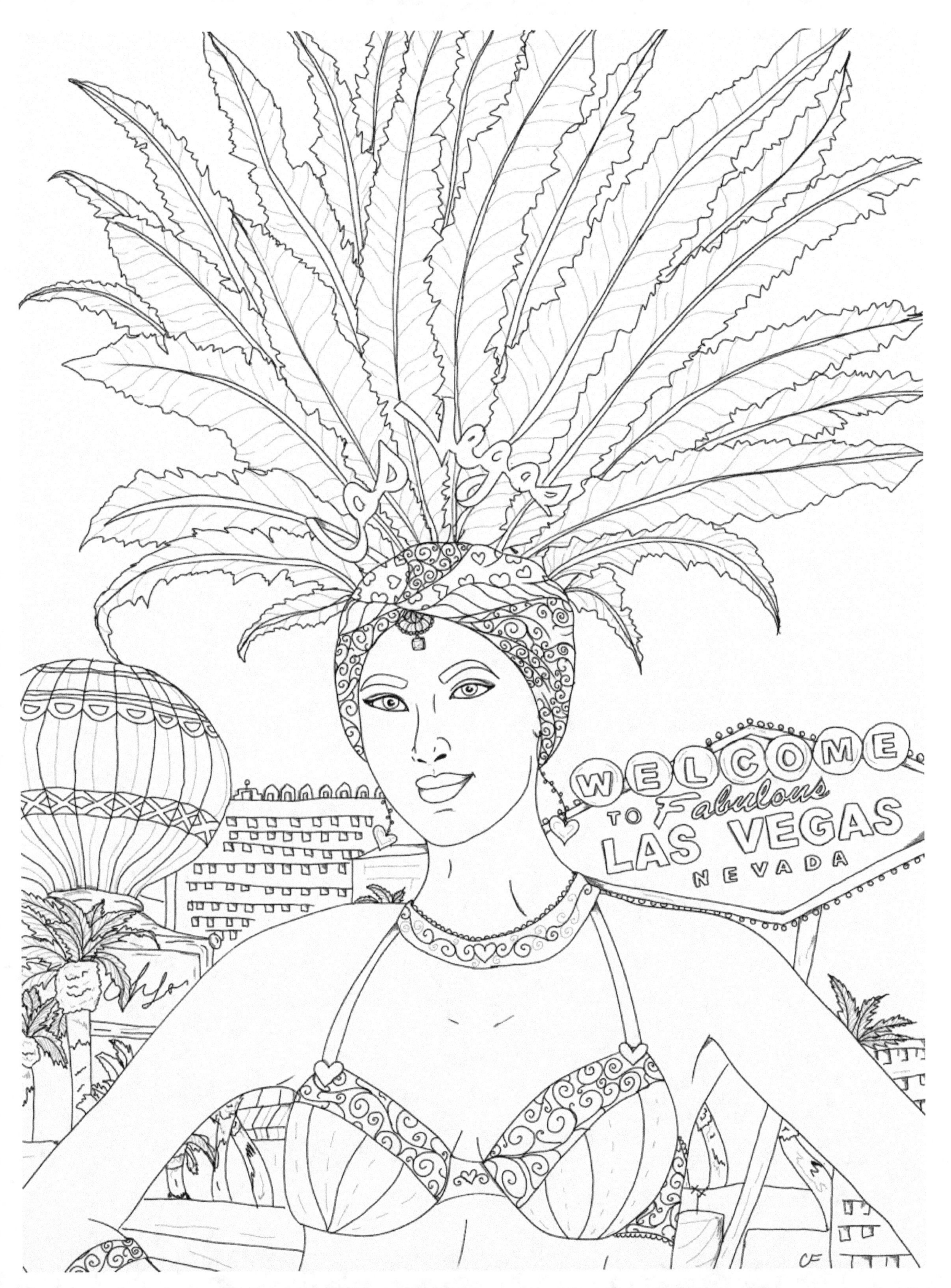

INSPIRED BY JAPAN

TEST COLORS HERE

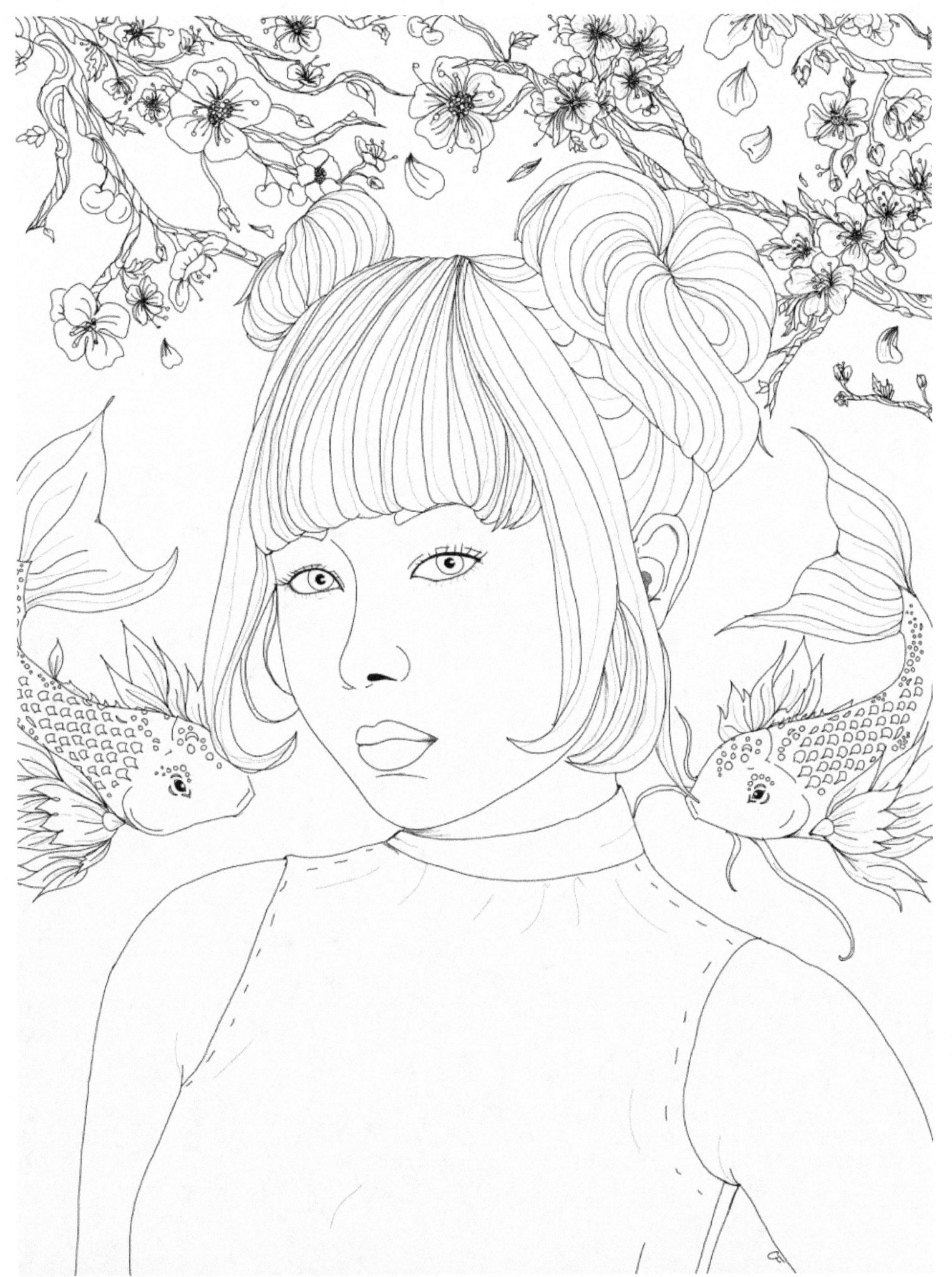

INSPIRED BY AUSTRALIA

TEST COLORS HERE

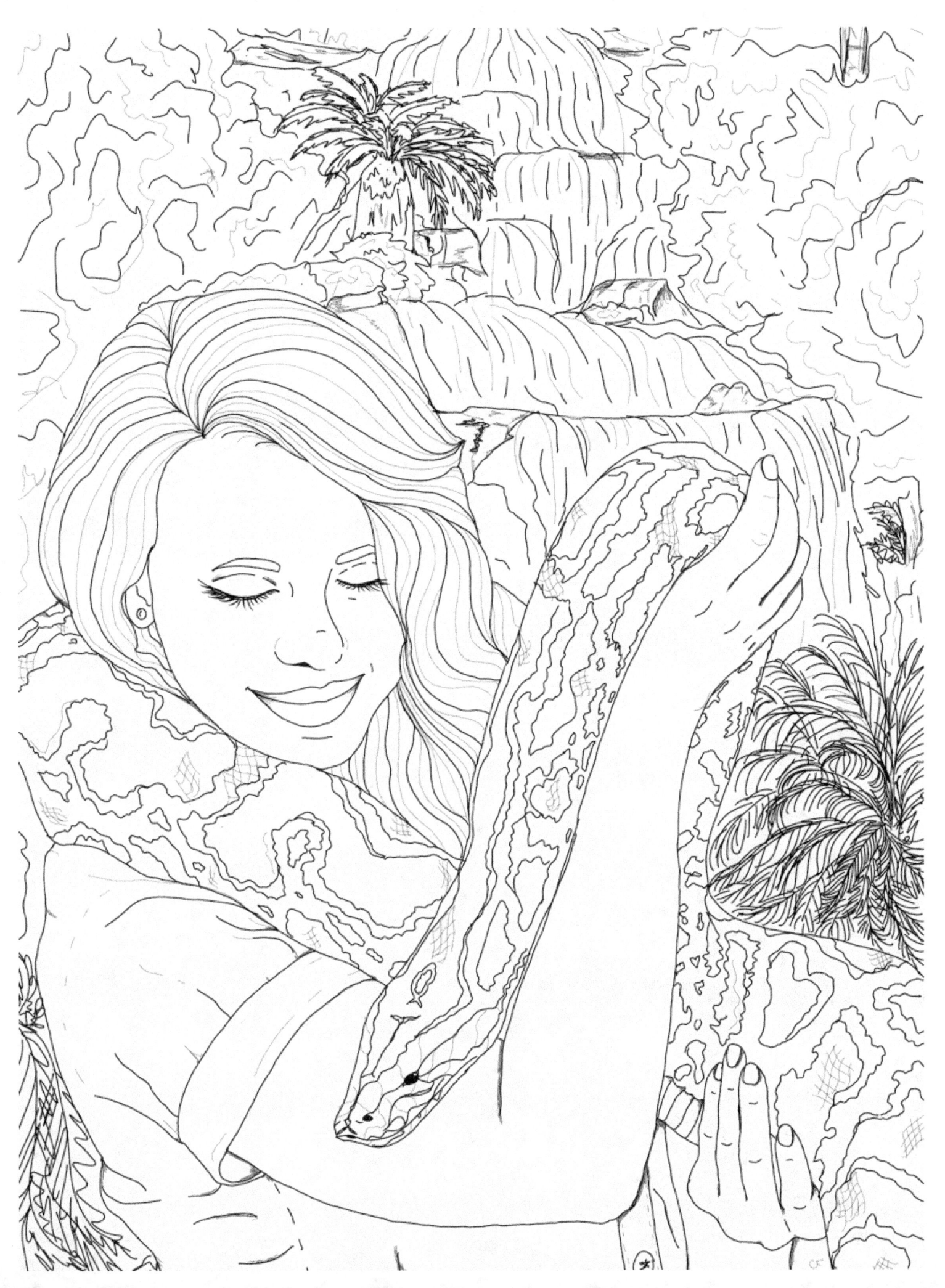

INSPIRED BY ENGLAND
TEST COLORS HERE

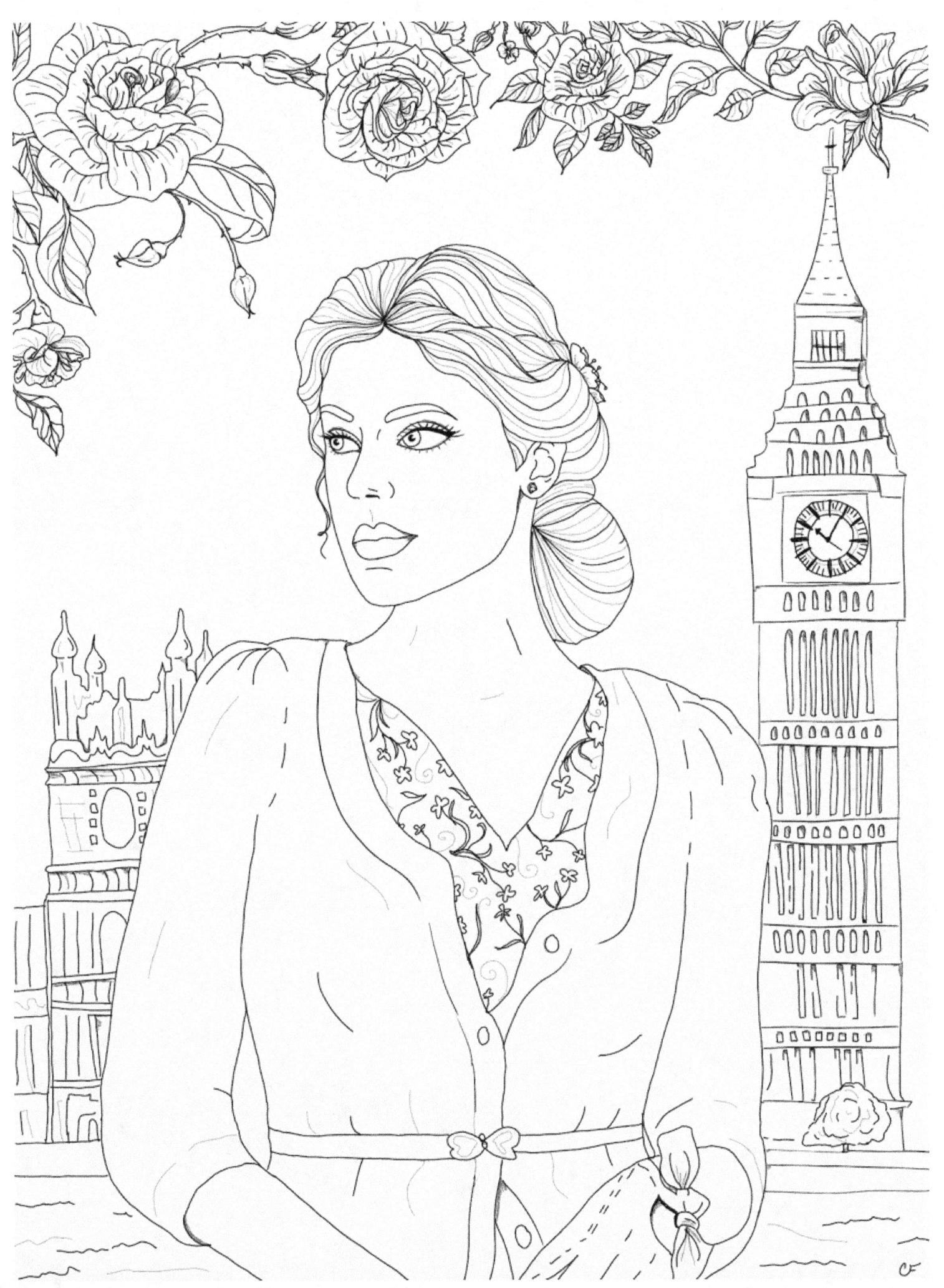

INSPIRED BY CHINA
TEST COLORS HERE

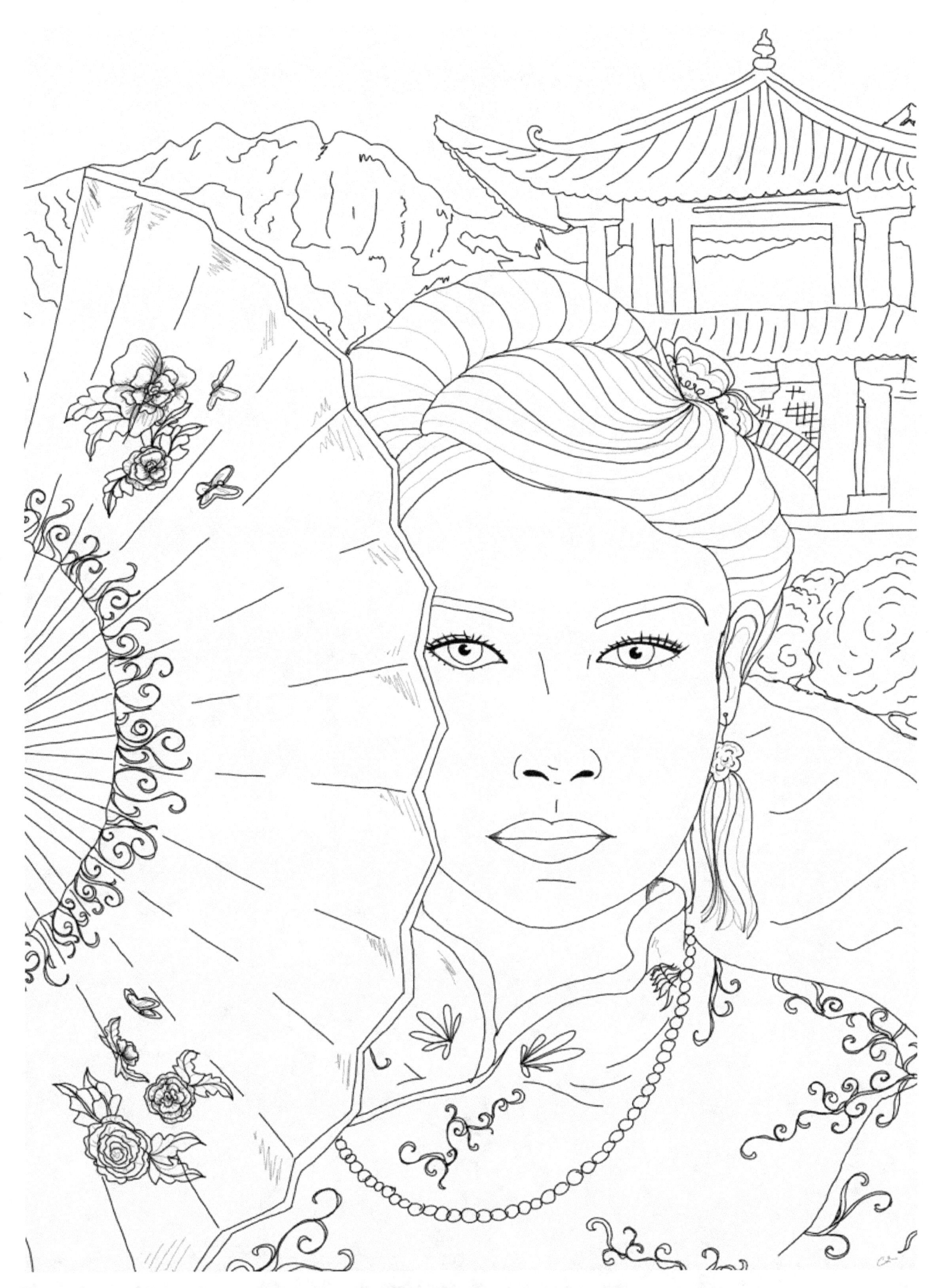

INSPIRED BY THE NETHERLANDS

TEST COLORS HERE

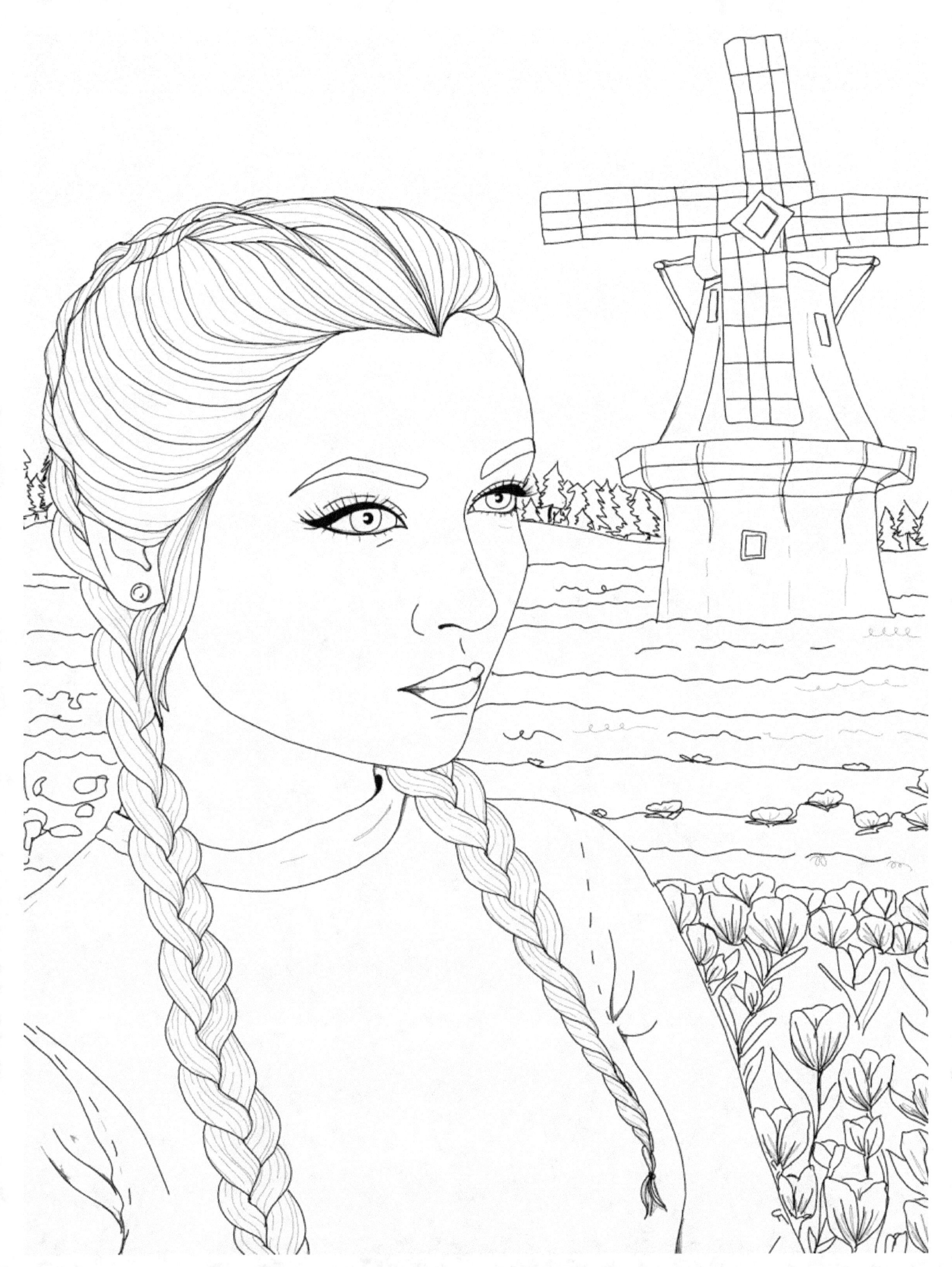

INSPIRED BY EGYPT

TEST COLORS HERE

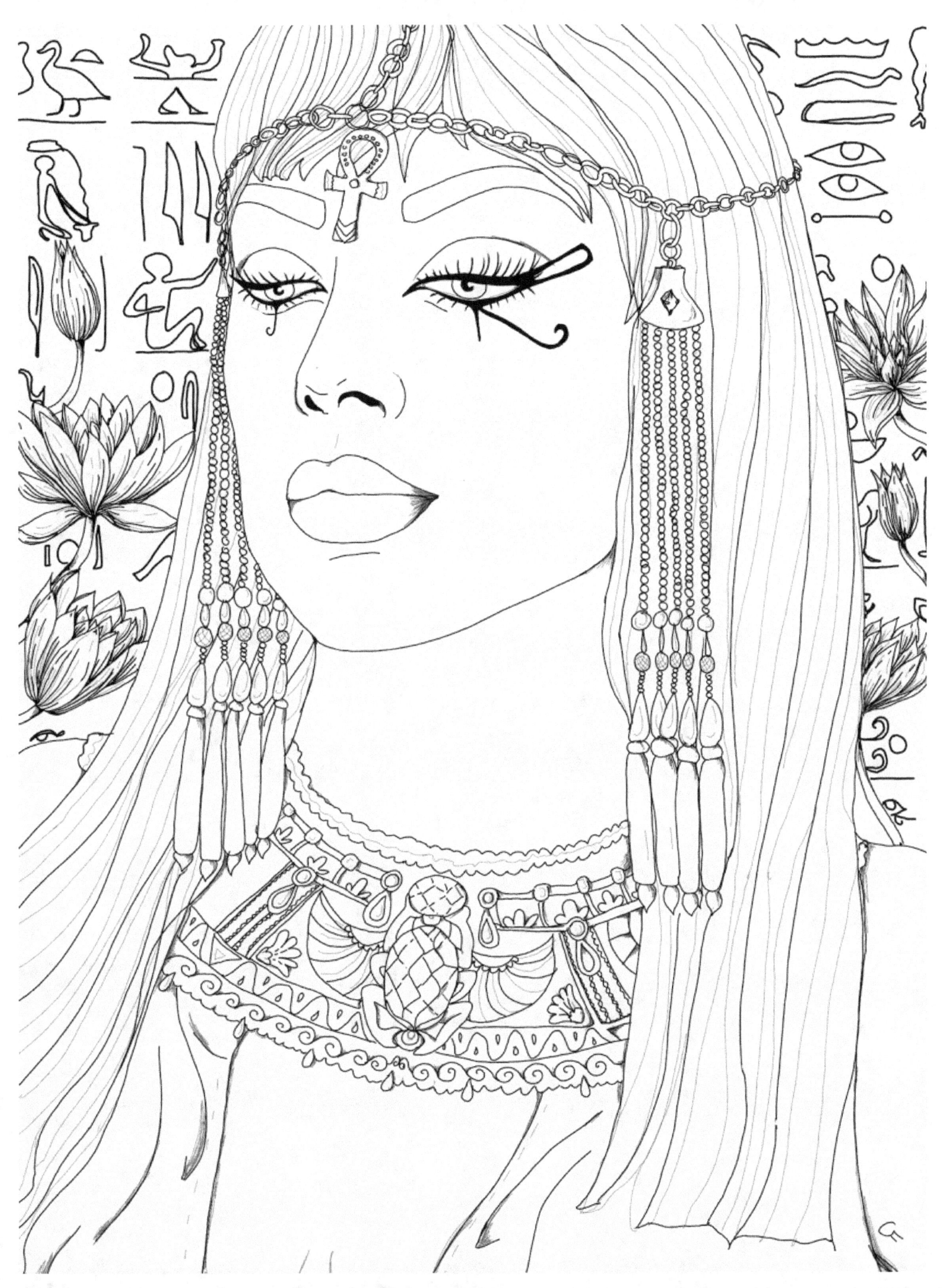

INSPIRED BY IRELAND

TEST COLORS HERE

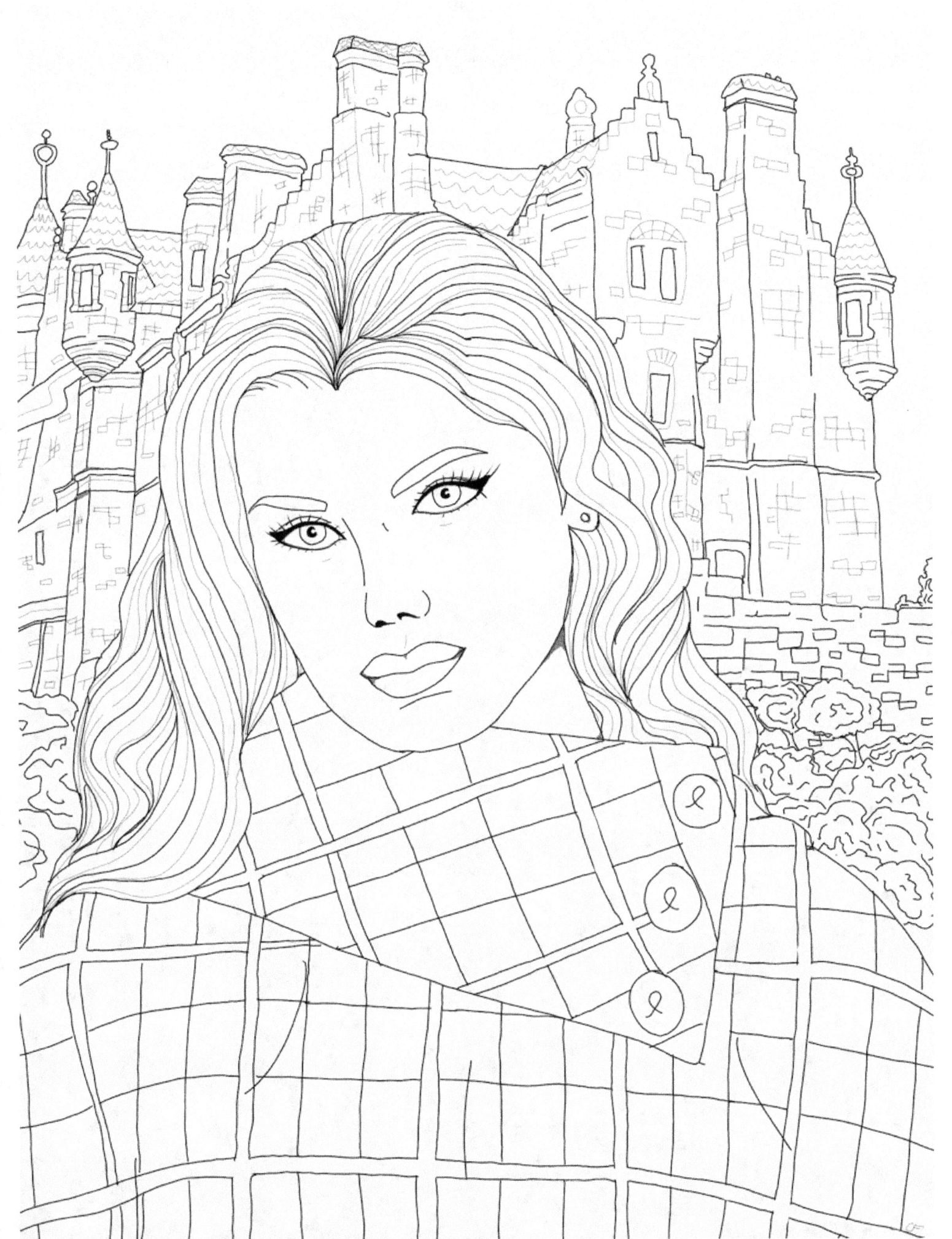

INSPIRED BY SPAIN

TEST COLORS HERE

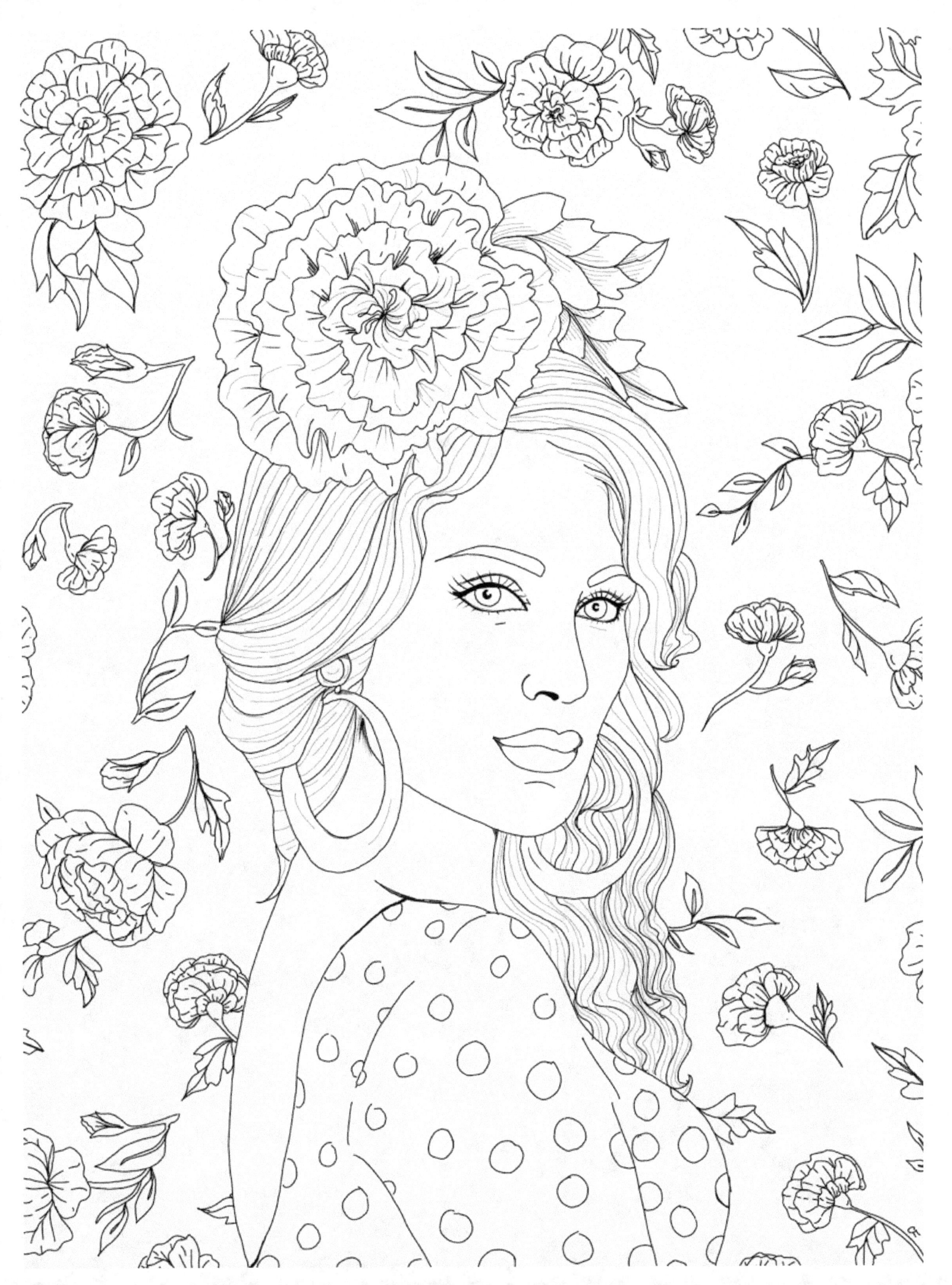

INSPIRED BY ALASKA, USA

TEST COLORS HERE

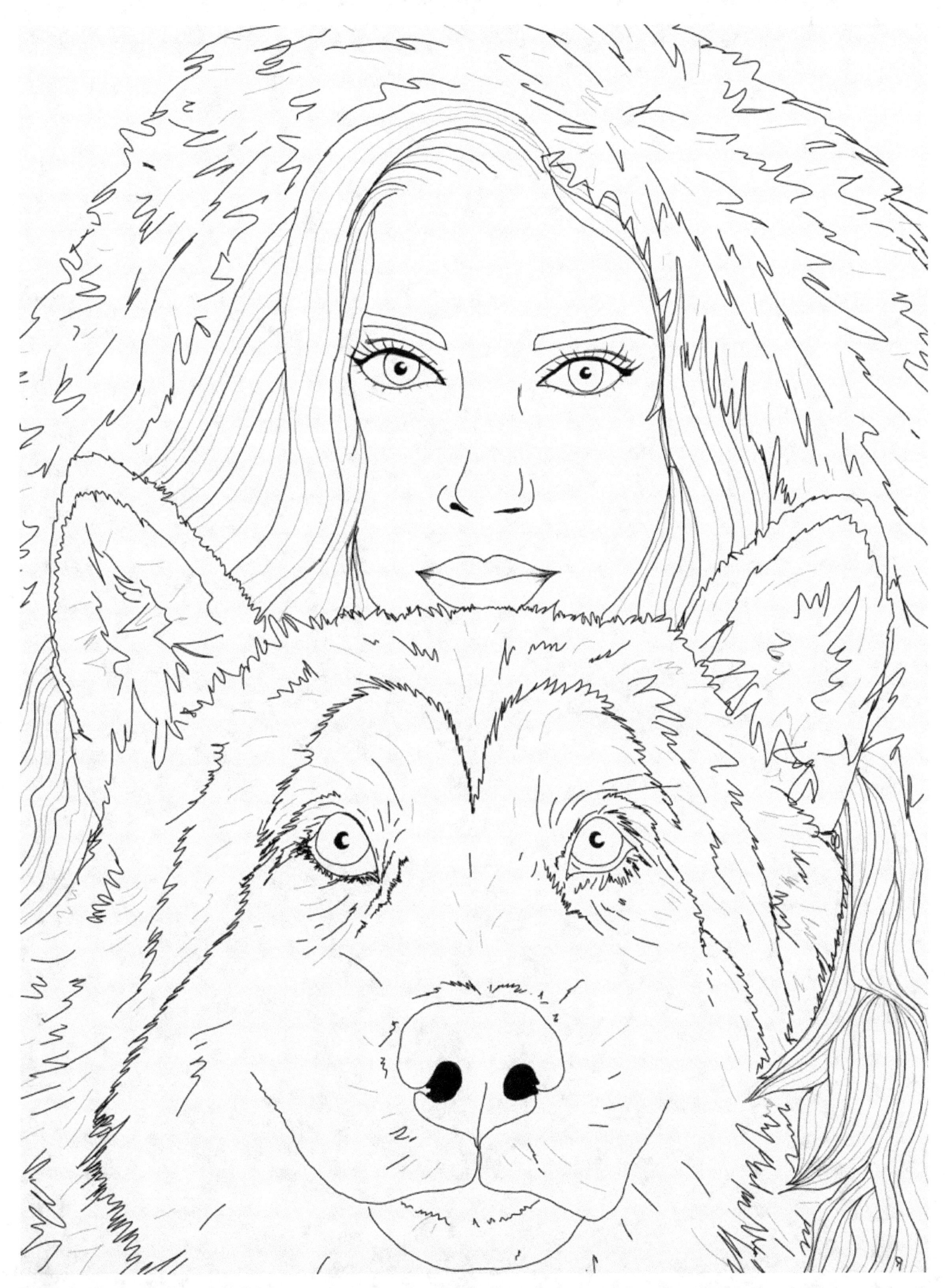

INSPIRED BY SAUDI ARABIA

TEST COLORS HERE

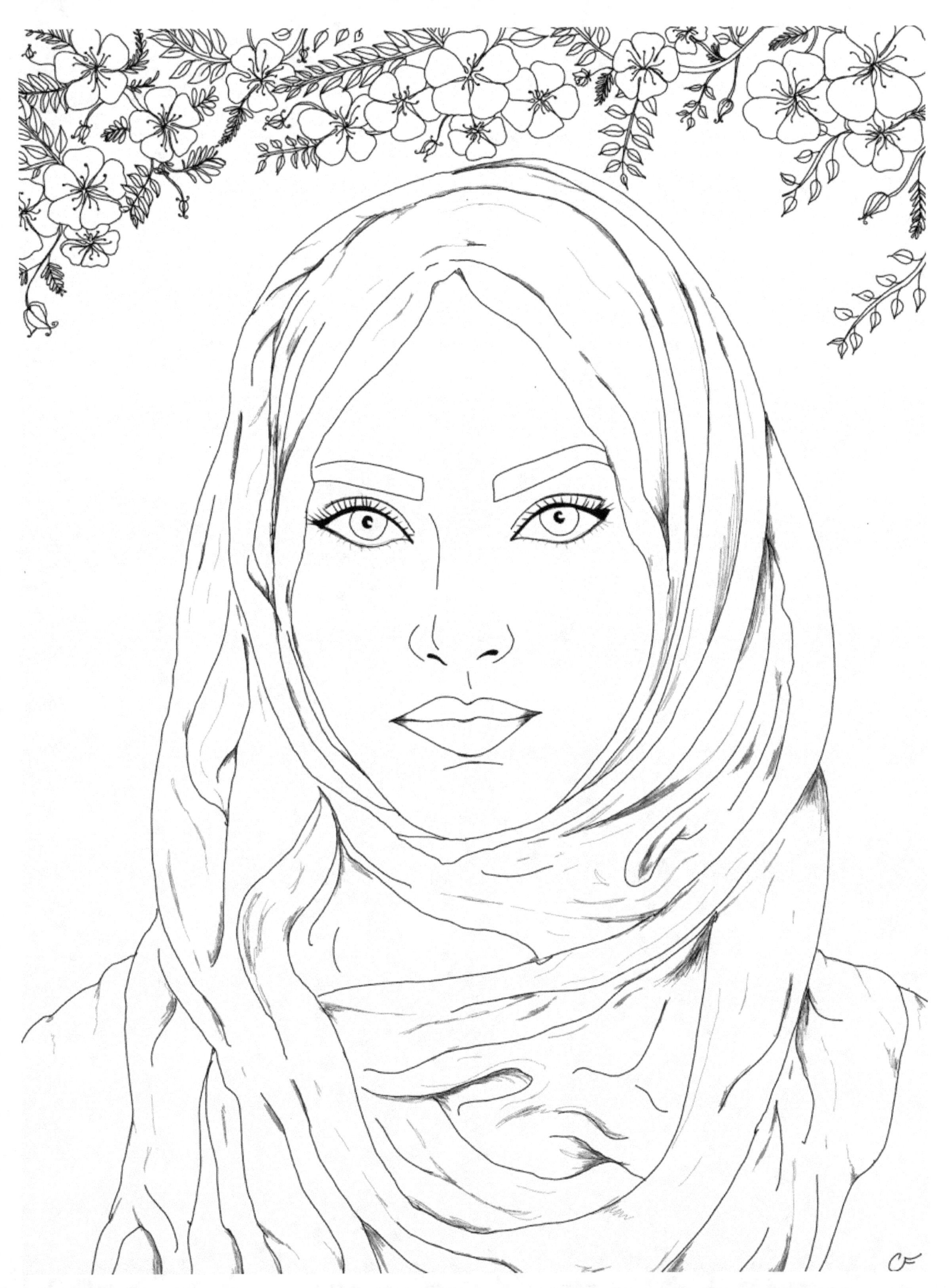

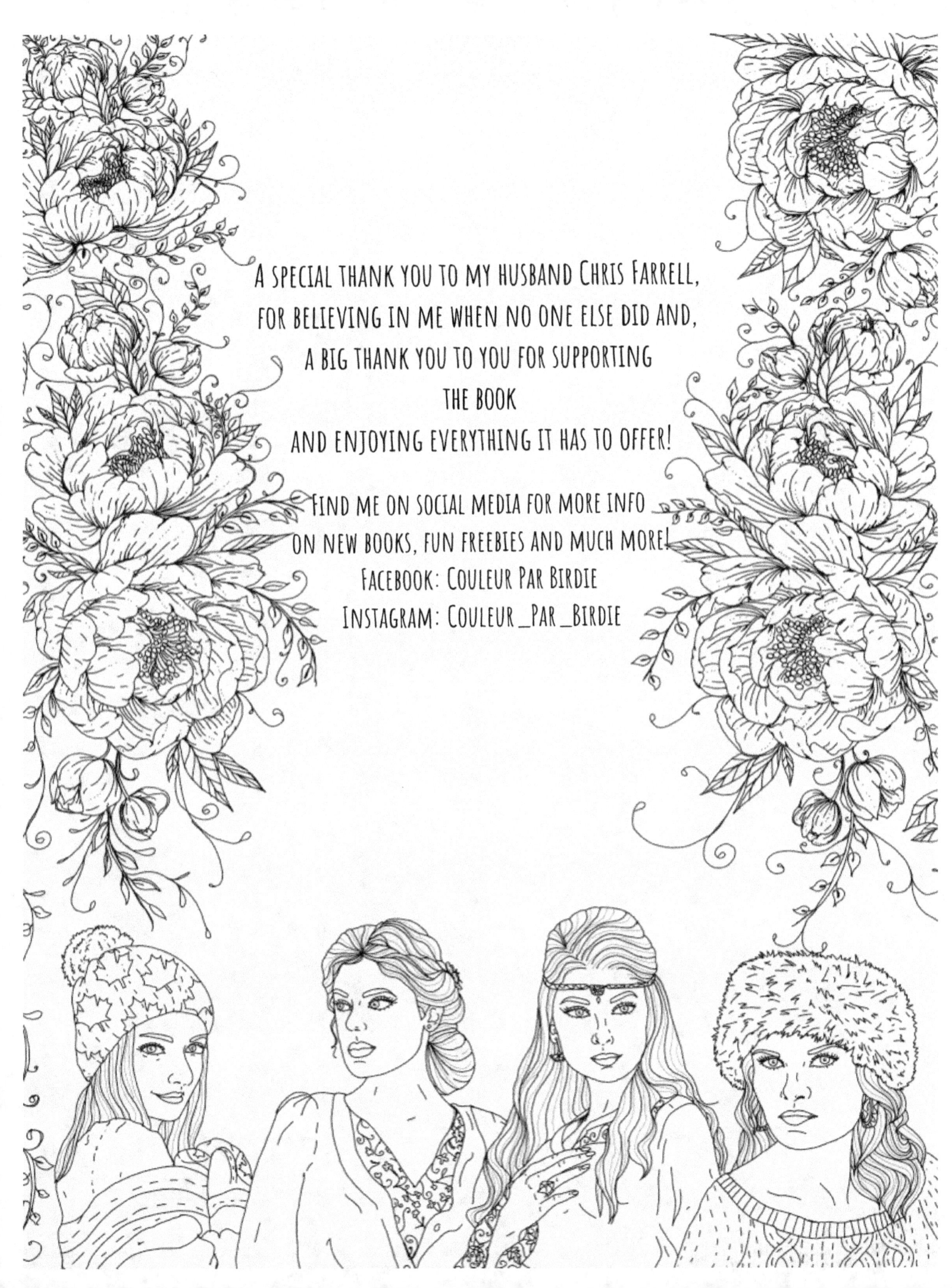

A special thank you to my husband Chris Farrell,
for believing in me when no one else did and,
a big thank you to you for supporting
the book
and enjoying everything it has to offer!

Find me on social media for more info
on new books, fun freebies and much more!
Facebook: Couleur Par Birdie
Instagram: Couleur _Par _Birdie

www.ingramcontent.com/pod-product-compliance
Lightning Source LLC
Chambersburg PA
CBHW081258180526
45170CB00007B/2482